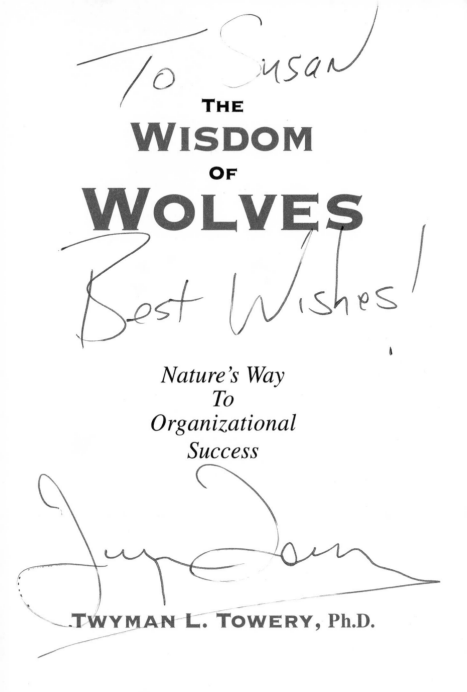

THE
WISDOM
OF
WOLVES

Nature's Way
To
Organizational
Success

TWYMAN L. TOWERY, Ph.D.

WESSEX HOUSE PUBLISHING
Brentwood, Tennessee

Copyright © 2000 by Twyman L. Towery
Jacket design and graphics by Gary Bozeman, Bozeman Design, Franklin, TN
Layout and typesetting by John Mitchell, MY Communications, Antioch, TN
Marketing director, Patricia H. Walker, Franklin, TN

Published by Wessex House Publishing
141 Rue de Grande
Brentwood, TN 37027
(615) 370-3587
Fax: (615) 661-8944
Website: www.twymantowery.com

Library of Congress Cataloging-in-Publication Data
Towery, Twyman L.
        The wisdom of wolves: nature's way to organizational success /
Twyman L. Towery
        p. cm.
ISBN 0-9646872-0-8 (hardcover : alk. Paper)
1. Success—Psychological aspects   2. Success in business   I. Title
BF637.S8T63 1997
158-dc21

                                                                    97-41429
                                                                    CIP

Printed and bound in the United States of America
10 9 8 7 6 5 4 3 2 1

In memory of my father,
Clarence Goodrich Towery,
who through his teaching and personal example
taught me, along with thousands of others,
to respect all living things.

CONTENTS

ACKNOWLEDGMENTS

Parker Sherrill of the Public Policy Planning Group: Your unwavering friendship epitomizes the Danish proverb that reinforces, "He who gives to me teaches me to give."

J. Franklin Bradley of Notch/Bradley: You've taught me that friends, no matter how far you think you are from them, are always close by when you really need them.

Randy McClain, owner of the White Wolf Gallery in Gatlinburg, Tennessee: This book reflects your zealous commitment, experience, and knowledge of wolves. Thanks.

Henry Berry, my literary agent: Without your perseverance and unwavering support, this project would not have been possible.

Laura Towery, my daughter: Your talent, patience, and understanding have always exceeded all of my expectations.

To some very special friends, including: Bo Roberts, Kathy Berlin, Bob and Patricia Hardison, Charles and Phyllis McLeroy, Kyle Viator, Tom Weiss, Paula Booten, and Garry Gause.

To these and countless others to whom I owe a great debt of gratitude and have not mentioned here: I pass along a sincere thank you for your time, advice, and talent.

WOLF CREDO

Respect the elders
Teach the young
Cooperate with the pack

Play when you can
Hunt when you must
Rest in between

Share your affections
Voice your feelings
Leave your mark

PREFACE

PREFACE

The original working title of this book was *The Wisdom Of Wolves & Men: Nature's Way To Organizational Success*. The term "men" was intended to be generic for all humans. One reason for this was that a term like "humankind" was simply too cumbersome and just did not sound right. There was also the underlying assumption that a book like this would be primarily of interest to men — businessmen, to be exact.

We could not have been more wrong on both counts. At least 10 of the first 12 women who test-read the manuscript for me exclaimed that they loved the book, and added jokingly, "How can you put the words 'men' and 'wisdom' in the same sentence?" I got their message that this was not a subject of interest only to men. The other part of my discovery was that the subject of this book has universal appeal, without regard to gender, social class, education, nationality, or age.

Audiences and readers everywhere relate to the spirit of the wolf because they find it to be relevant to their lives. These stories of wolves and humans are a combination of wisdoms that evoke an attitude organizations want to foster among their employees, as well as parents among their children.

The ideas that are embodied in this book were conceived at the end of a particularly grueling consulting assignment. When I arrived home late that Friday night, I felt depressed as I recalled the ingenious new ways that this particular group of corporate executives had discovered to one-up each other, lie to each other, and generally stab each other in the back. When I turned on public television to unwind, I was immediately in a different world, the milieu of the wolf pack, where teamwork, loyalty, and communication are the norm rather than the exception.

My overriding thought was "what could human organizations accomplish if they lived by these principles?" The next morning, I was at the library absorbing everything I could about wolves. Soon, I was in northern Minnesota answering the call of a wolf pack with a howl of my own, both literally and figuratively. The resulting stories of wolves and humans are used as metaphors to remind us that there is profound intelligence and knowledge in our universe other than that of humans.

Today, there is a resurgence of interest in wolves throughout the world. People want to know more about their old friend, realizing that we share a special bond. There is undoubtedly something in the human soul that enjoys a special relationship with one of the wolf's gifts to us, the dog. Dogs have become cherished members of peoples' families throughout the world. But dogs are not wolves.

Since the first printing of *The Wisdom Of Wolves*, I have received letters from people all over the world who wanted to share their experiences with wolves. For them, those moments are forever frozen in time. Through the kindness of people who love wolves, I have learned that some commonly accepted "truisms" about wolves are not necessarily true. For example, although never recommended, wolves have become harmonious members of a few human families, but the process began shortly after birth so their early life experience was with people. Humans, therefore, became their social group. The reason for this unlikely integration is simple — being an integral, respected, loved member of an organized social order is the most important thing in the life of a wolf. The wolf truly lives for the pack.

There are many reasons why people today are rediscovering the wonder ancient peoples felt toward wolves when they painted them on their stone walls so long ago, just as there are many reasons why the wolf was chosen as the symbol of so many Native American tribes. Today, we are coming to realize that wolves, perhaps like no other animal, represent the wild, untamed side of life that we, in our automated frenzy, yearn for more than ever.

Even though our lives have become extremely complex and sophisticated, it was not long ago that our ancestors were hunters and gatherers, living a life of coexistence with the wolf and the other animals. Today, our business and professional lives may thrive, while our family unit disintegrates before our very eyes. Technology dominates our lives, while our souls ache for understanding. In short, many of us simply do not know who we are anymore — we have lost our place and sense of purpose not only in nature's order but also among ourselves.

The wolf pack knows who it is. Those in the pack exist for each other. We long for this basic wisdom that has never eluded them. Many of us want to help our ancient partner return. After reading this book, I hope you will want to join us.

These quotes, stories, and anecdotes, whether from ancient or modern man, represent certain truths of the human experience. Some are serious and others, humorous. But when acknowledged and practiced, they can help us travel the elusive but timeless road to success and happiness.

Is there some principle of nature which states that we never know the quality of what we have until it is gone?

RICHARD HOFSTADTLER

Experience comes from what we have done, wisdom comes from what we have done badly.

THEADORE LEVITT

Don't accept your dog's admiration as conclusive evidence that you are wonderful.

ANN LANDERS

Never does Nature say one thing and Wisdom another.

JUVENAL

INTRODUCTION

Introduction

One of the primary questions facing us all today is: "Who's in charge here? Can we have control over happiness and success in our work, homes, and social life, or are we simply a twig trying to ride out a hurricane?"

The principles that assure happiness and success are as true today as they were centuries ago. Universal truths are not situational. Their correctness has been proven by the test of time. So too has the wolf pack proven the effectiveness of its organizational principles through the test of time.

For centuries, man and wolf coexisted, viewing each other more with awe than with fear. Each respected the other's social order and hunting skills. They were partners in maintaining the earth's intricate balance. They understood that they were a part of nature, rather than nature being a part of them.

Then man began to believe that he was superior and that

he no longer needed the wolf. In fact, he no longer even honored the wolf's right to exist. Bounties were offered to encourage the poisoning, shooting, and trapping of wolves everywhere. This was in spite of the fact that the wolf had given man his most loyal friend and working partner, the dog. Whether out of envy, fear, or ignorance, man set out to destroy the wolf, nature's mirror image of man in so many ways.

Though diminished, the wolf pack has persevered against all odds, protecting its successful family organization and social structure.

There is a growing recognition that we can once again learn from our ancient friend, Canis Lupus. Currently, the wolf is beginning, with man's assistance, to make a comeback in many parts of the world. Today the human social order seems to be falling apart, while the wolf family remains intact. Our organizations and the people within them are disoriented from the aftershocks of divorce, crime, overpopulation, reorganization, downsizing, mergers, and work redesign, while the organization of the wolf pack remains a model of playfulness, teamwork, efficiency, and sharing.

Our educational system is suffering a staggering decline, while the wolf pack, as always, puts the education, protection, parenting, and mentoring of their young first. They know that in their children lies their future, and they act accordingly. We obviously have much to learn from the wolf.

Everything is perfect coming from the hands of the creator; everything degenerates in the hands of man.

JEAN-JACQUES ROUSSEAU

Truth does not change because it is, or is not, believed by a majority of the people.

GIORDANO BRUNO

In nature, the emphasis is on what is rather than what ought to be.

HUSTON SMITH

Nature knows no indecencies; man invents them.

MARK TWAIN

ABOUT WOLVES

ABOUT WOLVES

There are some memories that become part of us. In my generation these often include John F. Kennedy's assassination, *Sputnik*, man's first walk on the moon, or Elvis Presley's death. For me, my first close-up wolf encounter belongs in that category. There is an old saying that wolves can see two looks away. They see deeper than we do and they anticipate our next action. I am a believer.

When I visited the International Wolf Center in Ely, Minnesota, I entered a room with a glass wall designed to allow viewing of the resident wolf pack. There were about 15 people in the room — men, women, and children. After I entered, my attention was riveted by a pair of beautiful, intense eyes fixed directly on me. I tried to meet the stare but could not. Then I looked away.

When I once again tried to return the stare, it occurred to

me that this was my first truly "personal" wolf encounter. This gorgeous Alpha male wolf seemed only interested in me. He engaged me in a way that was both unnerving and intimidating. The glass partition between us did not matter, for I was convinced that the wolf could see into my soul and interpret my aura. I still am.

Since then, as I have continually tried to learn more about wolves, I never cease to be amazed at the misconceptions people have about them, even in this age of enlightened communication. For instance, people who live in rural areas of the South often tell me about the wolves that live near their farms, often killing their cattle, chickens, and goats. In truth, there have not been any wolves in that part of the country for generations.

People want to believe that the wild, ancient wolf still touches their lives, but they can never quite connect the myth with reality. Still, their fantasies persist.

In the United States today, the only wolf packs existing in sizable numbers are found in Alaska and Minnesota. Very small numbers of wolves reside in a few other states such as Wisconsin, Michigan, Montana, Idaho, Wyoming, and Washington. The reintroduction of wolves into Yellowstone National Park is a great achievement, but the long-term results are yet to be known. Canada has an abundant wolf population.

Now that they have the vital protection of the Endangered Species Act, there is great debate about whether wolves should be introduced into other areas they once inhabited or allowed to return naturally, if possible. I cannot answer that question. This book is not meant to serve as an authoritative text on wolves. Many excellent resources already exist to fulfill that need — some of which are listed in the back of this book. However, some basic information will be helpful to anyone with even a casual interest in the subject.

Social Order

The social order of the wolf is very evolved, with an Alpha male and female as the leaders, a Beta male and female as second in command, and usually an Omega ranking at the bottom. The Alpha male possesses strength, hunting genius, decision-making ability, powerful personality, and great physical prowess. He is, literally, the leader of the pack. The Alpha female serves both as his mate and as co-leader of the pack. Her personality basically matches the Alpha male's personality. The survival of the pack depends upon their wisdom, judgment, and leadership.

The Alpha male and female constantly demonstrate their authority, never allowing the other wolves to "get out of their place." The Alpha male generally concentrates on keeping the other males in line, while the Alpha female dominates the other females. The Alpha male often demonstrates its dominance by snarling, snapping, chasing, biting, and standing over the other wolves. These "lessons" are not lost on the other pack members.

The Omega wolf is the scapegoat of the pack, eating last, bearing the blame for what goes wrong, and generally being an easy mark to pick on. While the Alpha wolves effortlessly communicate their authority, the Omega wolf is a picture of submissiveness as it lies on its back with its stomach up in a vulnerable position or walks with its tail between its legs. Every other wolf harasses the Omega wolf.

The rank of a wolf within the pack can often be determined by how it holds its tail. The tails of the Alpha wolves will be held high. The middle wolves' tails are held at a low position. The Omega wolf, as befits its status, will tuck its tail between his legs.

The actual size of a wolf pack (family) varies greatly, but will average around five to eight wolves. Wolves also vary in terms of their physical size and coloration, even within the same pack. The family of the gray wolf is actually made up of members with coats of many colors. They range from conservative gray to brown, tan, silver, and even flamboyant yellow and red. The territory this family calls home will average from a minimum of 25 square miles to around 150 miles. However, this range may increase to as much as 1,000 square miles in vast open areas such as Canada and Alaska.

Life and Death

Wolf pups weigh about one pound at birth, with the average litter consisting of five to six pups. The average adult female timber wolf weighs about 85 pounds, while the males weigh about 95 pounds. They stand about two feet tall and are five to six feet in length, from the tip of their nose to the end of their tails. In the wild, wolves may survive to 13 years of age, but most do not live past about nine years. However, in captivity, wolves often live past 15 years. Obviously, the life of the wild wolf is hard and fraught with danger. Approximately half of all wolves die before reaching one year of age. This heavy toll is taken by other predators, such as grizzlies and polar bears, and by factors such as inexperience, hunting accidents, and disease.

Fighting Among Wolves

A lot of growling, snarling, snapping, lurching, and scary curling of lips goes on within a wolf pack, but serious fights are very rare. Preferring peaceful communication to war, wolves let others know the boundaries of their territory by marking and howling. However, when the pack feels threatened by an intruding wolf pack, wolves are ferocious defenders of their turf.

Danger to Humans

Most wolves are not dangerous to people. No one on the

North American continent has ever been killed by a healthy wolf. In fact, wolves are very shy of people and do everything possible to stay out of our way. Only when a wolf is injured or diseased is it a genuine danger to humans.

Why Do We Need Wolves?

Wolves are important to maintaining a healthy, natural environment. They are carnivores (meat eaters), and by eating the weak, sick, old, and young of other animal populations, the wolf plays a vital role in controlling their numbers. If not for wolves, large animals that need great amounts of food, such as caribou, moose and deer, would damage the forest by overpopulation and decimation of plants and trees. Research shows that when wolves are removed from an area, the remaining big game often suffer starvation and disease. Eskimos and Native Americans observed that, without the wolf, the large animals they depended upon for survival became weak and diseased. They honored the wolf's presence.

After birthing their pups, wolves abandon their den site, which is often adopted as a home by porcupines or other smaller animals. Birds often scavenge the wolf fur left behind to help construct their nests. When wolves have had their fill and leave a carcass behind, many other animals such as ravens, coyotes, and foxes feast on their leftovers. In nature, nothing is wasted.

Most of all, though, we need wolves for the health of our

spirit. Wolves are the epitome of beauty, dignity, and intelligence. They are tough and hardy and can compete with practically anything on earth except guns, poison, and traps — in short, man. Their family order is second to none. Wolves are devoted to their family, and they show great sensitivity to the needs of the other members. Wolves are extremely loyal, and they lavish affection on their fellow pack members. The most wonderful entities in our world simply cannot be explained in bottom-line terms of dollars and cents, for their mystery is too complex and beautiful. This is why we need the wolf.

THE MYTH OF THE BIG BAD WOLF

THE MYTH OF THE BIG BAD WOLF

Who's afraid of the Big Bad Wolf? Until recently, apparently everybody. But a wave of education in recent years has allowed the wolf to capture the hearts of people from all walks of life. People everywhere have developed a keen fascination for the wolf pack and its virtues of teamwork, intelligence, loyalty, and communication skills. Groups of seminar attendees can be heard practicing the distinctive howl of the wolf — with each person being cautioned to respect the distinctness of every other person's howl, just as it is with the wolf pack.

There are many reasons for the almost paranoid fear humans have felt over time toward wolves. One possibility is that because a symbol of Christ is the lamb, and because lambs make a nice dinner for wolves, it is easy to portray the wolf as evil. The wolf, seen as the enemy of the lamb, has become the victim of negative symbolism throughout Western civilization.

During the Middle Ages, there undoubtedly were incidents involving wolves and people that led to an omnipresent fear of wolves throughout Europe. In Europe the close proximity of wolves and humans led to clashes over food and living space. However, it is likely that most of these skirmishes involved hybrid wolf/dog offspring, which were often rabid.

These hybrid species developed during the Middle Ages when it became " sheik" to have wolves by the side of rulers in the royal courts. The wolf's abilities as a great hunter and warrior of tremendous intelligence were characteristics a ruler hoped would be associated with him, so he wanted wolves at his court. European wolves, however, were not particularly large and were not as physically impressive as some breeds of large dogs, so wolves and dogs were purposefully mixed. These crossbreeding practices resulted in hybrids that were often unpredictable and ferociously aggressive. The hybrids soon escaped into the countryside where they attacked livestock and people, with wolves receiving the blame. Wolves were almost entirely exterminated in Europe, in part as a result of the fear of attack that continued to sweep the continent.

"Werewolf" stories are one derivative of the attitude humans formed toward wolves — reflecting a cold-blooded killer of men, women, and children of almost satanic proportions. In the past, people were tortured mercilessly and put to death because they were believed to be werewolves. Captured wolves were also hung and burned at the stake. A wolf's presence was equated with the presence of the devil, and if someone was perceived to have wolf qualities, then the devil was believed to reside within that person.

The fear of wolves is perpetuated by folklore and fairy tales as well. For example, the tale of Little Red Riding Hood has been interpreted by some as a sexual warning to adolescent girls. By speaking to the wolf, Red Riding Hood took the first step toward her ultimate destruction. The wolf was a symbol of evil, perhaps representing the devil who was there solely to tempt people.

We also associate wolves symbolically with war and dishonesty. Groups of deadly German submarines that patrolled the Atlantic and caused inestimable damage to the Allies were called "wolf packs." Hilter's retreat was known throughout the world as the "Wolf's Lair." An unprincipled womanizer is called a "wolf." A dangerous person with a pleasant appearance and easy personality is known as a "wolf in sheep's clothing." Let your imagination take over, and you can probably add several more examples to this list.

The same "manifest destiny" theory that settlers used to justify their slaughter of the Native American population was also invoked to eliminate the wolf. It was not enough to destroy them; they were slain with hate and vengeance. Wolves often were soaked with kerosene and burned alive. It was also considered great sport to wire their mouths shut and turn them loose to starve to death.

But today we are beginning to shed these myths and, fortunately, are changing our behavior toward this beautiful and mystic creature. We are starting to view the wolf as did the Native Americans, who respected them for their courage, intelligence, and tremendous skills. These people often clothed themselves in wolf heads and hides, hoping the magic of the wolf would enter their bodies and minds and that they could inherit its great skills and abilities.

Today, we know that we do not need a wolf hide — we can simply choose to let the lessons of the wolf pack guide our behavior toward others.

TEAMWORK

TEAMWORK

What a gorgeous sight! As wolves travel the vast horizons in search of their prey, they traverse the snow. One of their favorite methods of travel is single file, one directly behind the other. The lead wolf expends the most energy. He is the trailblazer, crashing through the soft snow, allowing each succeeding wolf to conserve energy. When the lead wolf tires, he may drop off to the side and allow the next wolf to assume the lead position. The former lead wolf can now trail the other pack members, laboring less and regaining his strength for the challenges yet to come.

While the wolf pack is led by an Alpha male and Alpha female, each wolf assumes a share of responsibility for the welfare of the pack. For example, after a litter of pups is born, an uncle will often assume the job of "chief baby-sitter" so the Alpha female can join the Alpha male on a honeymoon hunt, allowing her some respite from her motherly duties. Every member of the pack does not aspire to be the boss — some prefer to be steady hunters, caretakers, or scouts. But everyone has a crucial role to play.

From the early playful romping with elders, the wolf pup is carefully trained to assume his part of the leadership of the pack as if his life and that of the pack depend upon it. For they do. It is the same with successful organizations and families. Members must be prepared not only to carry their own load but also to assume greater leadership at any time. The viability of the organization may well depend upon it.

Wolves not only cooperate with each other but also may work in harmony with other species to reach mutually desirable goals, and sometimes just to have fun. The raven is a case in point. An expert, skilled observer from above, when the raven discovers wounded or dead prey, it often acts as a messenger, summoning the wolf and other ravens to the scene. The wolves can open the carcass, thus providing enough food for everybody for days to come.

While the wolf may make playful lunges at the wily bird, and the raven may peck the wolf's rump while he's feeding, the two not only coexist, but obviously enjoy an intricate partnership forged from nature's law of efficiency and thousands of years of experience.

There is also a more intricate, less definable type of

teamwork in which wolves are key participants. It is exemplified by their successful introduction into Yellowstone National Park after years of research, planning, political perseverance, and masterful execution by literally thousands of people from all different strata of our society. Once released, the wolves have more than done their part — they have not only survived but have prospered and procreated beyond even the most optimistic projections. While there have been problems involved in this delicate operation, they have been much less significant than expected, and many formerly dubious ranchers have become staunch supporters of this reintroduction program.

Not only has the teamwork of the wolves among themselves been critical to their success, but the teamwork between humans and wolves has helped boost the life environment for both species.

The thrill felt by millions of people knowing that this great predator once again roams the vast expanse of Yellowstone is immeasurable. This great success story gives at least one positive sign for a future in which humans and wolves may coexist. Indeed, it is an apt metaphor for the kind of teamwork you and your company may need with your vendors, suppliers, distributors, and even your competitors.

A company is like a ship; everyone ought to be prepared to take the helm.

MORRIS WEEKS

No member of a crew is praised for the rugged individuality of his rowing.

RALPH WALDO EMERSON

There is no limit to what you can do if you don't care who gets the credit.

UNKNOWN

Individual commitment to a group effort — that is what makes a team work, a company work, a society work, a civilization work.

VINCE LOMBARDI

Teamwork is like the weather — everyone talks about it, but often nobody does anything about it. It is seldom achieved by intellectualizing; rather, it is the practical application of attitude, common goals, and experience working together. It is a learned art.

After *Sputnik*, American space workers were challenged like never before to put a man on the moon before the Russians. They became obsessed with victory. They achieved success through the skillful application of the team concept. Like America's space workers, people working together as teams can achieve goals they never before dreamed possible.

Business

In your organization must a crisis occur before people will effectively work together? If so, how can you replace this crisis syndrome with a proactive attitude?

Family

Many of us who are great team members at work take off our teamwork hats when we walk in the door at home. We do not seem to realize that our spouse and children are not nearly as interested in our job title as our taking time to relate to them as equals. Are you guilty of this? How would they want you to act differently?

Personal

Are you cut out to be a team player or do you really want to fly solo? Do you know the difference? Are you being true to yourself and to those with whom you work and live?

PATIENCE

PATIENCE

Except for man, wolves may be the most studied of animals. They have been observed and electronically monitored following herds of their prey for days. Amazingly, they never appear bored or weary of their task. They do not aimlessly chase or harass their prey. They seem content to remain keen observers, synthesizing and analyzing the physical condition and mental state of each member of the herd they are pursuing.

Of course, the weak, injured, young, and old of their prey are obvious targets. But the wolf's mastery goes much deeper than just identifying the easy victims. Wolves observe and record many minuscule personality traits and habits that we humans never perceive.

It may be a slightly nervous behavior or idiosyncrasy that makes an animal vulnerable; certain unique personality traits that prod an animal to leave the security of the pack and become an easy mark. These actions are all carefully noted by the watchful, patient wolf.

Wolves and caribou have a unique relationship, often beginning in the same birthing grounds and then traveling together over vast ranges through some of the most inhospitable geography on earth. Their relationship is not constantly adversarial, for they often seem to mingle among each other with seemingly little tension. But the moment does come.

Imagine this scene as described by a veteran wolf observer: a pack of wolves (drivers) suddenly rushes the caribou, causing them to run together as a herd for safety, while one of the pack's wolves (slasher) cuts diagonally across the caribou at a perpendicular angle, slicing the leg of a "designated" caribou, probably picked because of some particular vulnerability the pack has identified. The caribou is then allowed to return to the herd.

This scene is repeated time after time, day after day, as the wolves patiently bide their time while the wounded caribou loses blood, strength, and the will to resist. The wolves regularly change roles, with different wolves performing the role of slasher. Each new slash adds to the others, and the wolves' inevitable victory becomes ever more certain with each passing day. Finally, when the caribou is debilitated and no longer a serious threat to the wolves, they attack.

Victory is eventually theirs because of their patience. In fact, the wolves are extremely hungry, maybe near starving throughout this ordeal, which can take several days to reach its conclusion. Why don't they simply attack and be done with it? Because one well-placed hoof of an animal the size of a caribou will kill or render helpless the much smaller wolf. The wolf pack seeks long-term victory rather than short-term success.

Songs and legends of ancient peoples often celebrate the incredible skills of the wolf. It is the observation, singleness of purpose, teamwork, curiosity, attention to detail, and unrelenting patience that make the wolf successful.

These have also been characteristics of humans in earlier times. Are we losing these abilities? If so, can we reclaim them?

Never think that God's delays are God's denials. Hold on; hold fast; hold out. Patience is genius.

COMTE DE BUFFON

Patience is the ability to let your light shine after your fuse has blown.

BOB LEVEY, *THE WASHINGTON POST*

This would be a fine world if all men showed as much patience all the time as they do while they're waiting for fish to bite.

VAUGHAN MONROE

Nature thrives on patience; man on impatience.

PAUL BOESE

When we truly believe that fulfillment lies in the journey and not the outcome, we are on our way to mastering the art of patience. The essence of patience is to accept the natural rhythm of life and not attempt to make it adhere to our human-imposed timetable. It will not, and for that, we should be glad.

Business

How do we remind ourselves to observe, listen, and see what is going on in our organization? Do we believe that nature's principles operate in business units as well as among animals and in forests? Would "patience" be a virtue our business colleagues would associate with us?

Family

Many of us take out the frustration of our work life on those who truly love us, without recognizing the pain we are inflicting. When was the last time you were impatient with a family member? Did you explain or apologize? What can you do to stop and be more patient next time?

Personal

Patience is not inherited. It is an art, an attitude, a way of dealing with the world that is available to all of us. What do you need to do to become a patient person? How will you know when you have gotten there? What benefits will you realize?

UNITY THROUGH UNIQUENESS

UNITY THROUGH UNIQUENESS

There is not a more eerie, mournful, frightening, or beautiful sound at night than the musical extravaganza of a howling wolf pack. Campers and hunters who have heard this chorus are filled with wonder but are also usually immobilized by fear. Because of the melody of voices, it often sounds like they are surrounded by scores of wolves.

In truth, there are usually no more than five to eight wolves howling in a pack. The secret is that the wolves are always careful not to duplicate each other. Each wolf assumes a unique pitch, respecting the distinctiveness of the other members of the pack. While the notes may change, as in any beautiful song, one wolf will not copy the pitch of another.

Interestingly, this respect for the individual only

emphasizes the true unity of the group. They are one, but they are individuals, each contributing to the organization in their own unique way. Every wolf has his own voice. Every wolf respects the voice of every other wolf.

While no one knows for sure why wolves sing, nature has blessed them with a talent they have perfected through the generations. However, we can make some educated guesses about the phenomenon; they are happy, excited, playful, territorial, sorrowful, or simply reaffirming the spirit and unity of their pack. After all, why do birds sing? Why do we?

An additional reason that wolves may howl is that it provides a time, a place, and an event for all social barriers to be broken. Wolves have a strong social order, with each member understanding its role and place. When we observe wolves eating together, we see what seem to be curtsies, bows, whines, and hugs — all according to each member's "place" in the organization. But when wolves howl together, all barriers are dropped, as if to say, "We are one, but we are all unique, so don't tread on us." As anyone who has ever listened to this magical howling choir will testify, its message is heard.

The wolf symphony makes the pack appear a much more formidable foe than would be the case if they all sounded the same. No wonder intruders become confused and frightened at what they assume to be an army of wolves.

So, too, are human organizations and families more

formidable when the awareness of each individual is celebrated rather than stifled. Each person assumes his share of responsibility for the group by employing his special talents and strengths. By members expressing their own uniqueness and respecting and encouraging the uniqueness of others, the unit becomes a strong, formidable one.

For the strength of the Pack is the Wolf, and the strength of the Wolf is the Pack.

RUDYARD KIPLING

When spider webs unite, they can tie up a lion.

ETHIOPIAN PROVERB

How much finer things are in composition than alone.

RALPH WALDO EMERSON

We must learn to live together as brothers or perish together as fools.

MARTIN LUTHER KING, JR.

Over the years I've learned a lot about coaching staffs and one piece of advice I would pass along to a young head coach — or a corporate executive, or even a bank president — is this: Don't make them in your image. Don't even try. My assistants don't look alike, think alike, or have the same personalities. And I sure don't want them thinking like I do. You don't strive for sameness, you strive for balance.

BEAR BRYANT

If a house be divided against itself, that house cannot stand.

MARK 3:25

Almost every kid lives for summer vacation. Funny skits, scary snakes, mountains of food, leaky canoes, practical jokes, blistering hikes, and most of all, the thrill of belonging, being part of a group.

It was the same every summer for me. Within hours of meeting my new cabin mates, we had decided we were the best team in camp-maybe the best in the camp's history. We were honor bound by some mysterious code to prove we were outstanding.

Though I rarely considered my own gifts, I did appreciate the talents of others. Tom could build a campfire in a creek. Perry could locate a spring in a desert. Jerry was a gourmet cook before we knew what the word gourmet meant. My specialty was spinning tales to make everybody laugh, or be scared (me included), or believe that together we could move a mountain. We were all different, but we made a great team.

Man, I loved summer camp.

Business

Interdepartmental teams (TQM, CQI, focus groups, etc.) are now utilized worldwide to constantly improve products, services, and customer awareness. Unfortunately, these teams are often formed without regard to the psychological makeup of the team members. Outstanding teams consist of individuals with differing gifts. There are several ways to enhance team selection, such as the use of the Myers Briggs Type Indicator (MBTI), which I frequently administer to groups. How do you make sure your team members will bring out the best in each other?

Family

Do you believe in birth order differences among children? Is it true that most people are tougher on their first born, more indecisive with the middle children, and easiest on the baby? Do you respect and enjoy your family members' differences, or do you try to force them to fit your preconceived mold?

Personal

We all possess unique gifts. We can either contribute these gifts toward the success of our work team and family, or we can use our uniqueness as an excuse to remain aloof and weaken the unit. What are your special contributions? How are you using them?

CURIOSITY

CURIOSITY

The world is a source of constant amazement to wolves. They take nothing for granted, preferring instead to investigate themselves. Nature's inanimate objects become their personal playthings — the rediscovered bone of a caribou, an antler, a buffalo chip, a pinecone, or even a camper's backpack and its contents. Every situation promises wonder, discovery, and surprise.

Their games are not unlike those of young human children — wrestling, pouncing on each other in ambush from behind rocks or trees, chasing each other in endless varieties of the game of hide-and-seek, gaining more confidence with every win.

Like human children, wolf pups' curiosity and games can often lead them into danger before they realize it. This is why the more experienced eye of the mature wolf is usually not far away.

A man who has done extensive research work in Alaska recently related to me how he was once making his rounds to collect data from different stations when an interesting event took place that illustrated the strong curiosity possessed by wolves. He got off his snowmobile and started to retrieve his data when he had an overwhelming sense that he was not alone. As he slowly turned his head, shivers of fear catapulted throughout his body, and he broke into a sweat despite the sub-zero weather.

Staring directly at him through a grove of trees was a pack of six wolves. He remembered how frighteningly beautiful they were as they blended into the landscape and the falling snow. They didn't move, and he couldn't move. When he finally recovered enough to remount his machine and take off, he looked behind and the wolves were still staring him down. About an hour and a half and several miles later, the man stopped at another station, started to retrieve his data, and was once again immobilized by a feeling of not being alone. Sure enough, when he looked behind him, there were the gray ghosts, riveting him with their stares.

This same sequence of events happened throughout the day until the researcher finally returned to his base camp. He said he had grown so accustomed to the wolves by then that he expected them to follow him on in, but he later realized that they knew the wilderness was their world, but the camp was his. Throughout the day, the pack showed great curiosity in him and his snowmobile as well. They never threatened or were aggressive in any way. Though the wolves appeared at each stop, the man never once saw them as he was traveling. The wolves were simply curious. They learned something that day. They always do.

Wolves are so curious about their environment that no matter how much they must hunt (for they are among the most tireless of hunters), we cannot help but observe that they hunt (work) in order to live (play, socialize).

These are their priorities.

What are yours?

What I know doesn't impress me . . . what I don't know excites me.

JEAN-JACQUES ROUSSEAU

Curiosity is one of the permanent and certain characteristics of a vigorous intellect

SAMUEL JOHNSON

The man who cannot wonder is but a pair of spectacles behind which there is no eye.

THOMAS CARLYLE

Curiosity is the wick in the candle of learning.

WILLIAM ARTHUR WARD

Harry Chapin sang a song that described a young boy who was unabashedly curious about how things might be. He experimented in class by painting flowers many different colors and told his teacher how he was able to see all the different colors in the rainbow in them. But his teacher repeatedly chastised him and drummed into him that "flowers are red, young man; leaves are green. There is no need to see flowers any other way than the way they always have been seen." Finally beaten down, he no longer saw nature's infinite possibilities and began following his teacher's instructions to the letter.

Later, his family moved to another city, and the boy's new teacher encouraged him to utilize his natural curiosity and realize possibilities rather than absolutes. It was too late: "Flowers are red and leaves are green," he told the teacher. Period. He had learned the misguided message all too well. The flame of his curiosity had been extinguished.

Business

Curious, creative employees often provide their employers more challenges, sometimes translated as difficulties. However, the inquisitive ones also offer greater opportunities for success. Do you play it safe or constantly explore the possibilities and test the limits in your work? How?

Family

The truly curious child can sometimes be a handful, taxing even the most patient of parents. However, there is usually a substantial payoff for this restless curiosity. Do you believe that curiosity nurtures creativity or simply that it "kills the cat"? Which attitude do you nourish among your family members?

Personal

What has amazed you today? What question would you like answered? How are you using your intelligence in unique and creative ways? Or do you stifle your curiosity, considering it troublesome and risky?

ATTITUDE

ATTITUDE

The attitude of the wolf can be summed up simply: It is a constant visualization of success. The collective wisdom of wolves has been progressively programmed into their genetic makeup throughout the centuries. Wolves have mastered the technique of focusing their energies toward the activities that will lead to the accomplishment of their goals.

Wolves do not aimlessly run around their intended victims, yipping and yapping. They have a strategic plan and execute it through constant communication. When the moment of truth arrives, each understands his role and understands exactly what the pack expects of him.

The wolf does not depend on luck. The cohesion, teamwork, and training of the pack determine whether the pack lives or dies.

There is a silly maxim in some organizations that

everyone, to be a valuable member, must aspire to be the leader. This is personified by the misguided CEO who says he only hires people who say they want to take his job. Evidently this is supposed to ensure that the person has ambition, courage, spunk, honesty, drive — whatever. In reality, it is simply a contrived situation, with the interviewee jumping through the boss's hoop. It sends warnings of competition and one-upmanship throughout the organization rather than signals of cooperation, teamwork, and loyalty.

Everyone does not strive to be the leader in the wolf pack. Some are consummate hunters or caregivers or jokesters, but each seems to gravitate to the role he does best. This is not to say there are not challenges to authority, position, and status-there are. But each wolf's role begins emerging from playtime as a pup and refines itself through the rest of its years. The wolf's attitude is always based upon the question, "What is best for the pack?" This is in marked contrast to us humans, who will often sabotage our organizations, family, or business if we do not get what we want.

Wolves are seldom truly threatened by other animals. By constantly engaging their senses and skills, they are practically unassailable. They are masters of planning for the moment of opportunity to present itself, and when it does, they are ready to act.

Because of training, preparation, planning, communication,

and a preference for action, the wolf's expectation is always to be victorious. While in actuality this is true only 10 percent of the time or less, the wolf's attitude is always that success will come — and it does.

When someone asked Abe Lincoln what he was going to do about his enemies after he was elected president, he replied, "I am going to destroy them. I am going to make them my friends."

ANONYMOUS

Get the right perspective. When Goliath came against the Israelites, the soldiers all thought, "He's so big we can never kill him." David looked at the same giant and thought, "He's so big, how can I miss?"

RUSS JOHNSON

People with a negative attitude brighten the whole room when they leave.

ANONYMOUS

Things turn out best for the people who make the best of the way things turn out.

JOHN WOODEN

Colonel Sanders was living out of the back of his car and seldom knew how he was going to get by from day to day. Franchising was a new concept, and people were suspicious of his plans for a far-reaching chain of restaurants. Besides that, most folks thought that at the Colonel's age, he should be retiring instead of trying to start a new business. He was certain of only one thing, that he knew how to make the best fried chicken in the world. His attitude was that since his Kentucky Fried Chicken was the best, success was only a matter of time.

Business

Do you really believe your product or service is the best? As a consumer, would it be your choice over all of your competitors? If not, what can you do about it? If the answer is nothing, shouldn't you think about making a change?

Family

Your family takes its cues from you. If you are confident, so are they. If you expect failure, so do they. If you are insecure, they are anxious. Do you leave your winning attitude at work, or do you share it with the ones you love? You do have a choice. But isn't this a choice only you can make?

Personal

Thinking positive is among the simplest sounding of concepts, but for most of us it is extremely difficult to consistently implement. A positive attitude requires more than reading motivational books or listening to "pump-you-up" speeches. It necessitates substance, which springs from a deep-rooted personal faith, a belief, a philosophy. What is yours? Can you express it to your family and business colleagues?

FAILURE

FAILURE

While the wolf pack may be nature's most effective hunting machine, it has a failure rate of approximately 90 percent. In other words, statistically, only one time out of 10 does the wolf have a successful hunt, which is so necessary to the survival of the pack. As a result, wolves are often hungry.

Their response is not lethargy, surrender, or defeat. They don't brood or go into depressive funks as people often do. Wolves simply rededicate themselves to the task at hand. They continue to apply their time-tested skills, utilizing the knowledge they have recently acquired from temporary setbacks, confident that success will eventually come. They never stop doing the little things, attending to every detail as they canvass endless miles each year in search of prey.

The human concept of failure has no relevance to the wolf. An unsuccessful hunt simply hones the skills and replenishes the desire. The mistakes made are not viewed as failures but instead become parts of the wolf's collective knowledge base. It is like entering data into a computer — the knowledge will be there for use in the future. What humans choose to consider failure, the wolf converts into wisdom.

Wolves seem to prioritize the unsuccessful events in their lives. Nine hunts that yield no results do not deter them, for they know that with the tenth or eleventh or even twelfth, victory will be theirs. These unsuccessful hunts are not failures — such as when a wolf gets careless and allows a moose hoof to hit him in the head and send him to the happy hunting ground. Now *that* is failure!

Many people view a single "unsuccessful hunt" as a symbol of their failure in life. From the wolf we learn that it is simply time to go hunting again. Failure is an attitude, not a reality. Failure is a perception; success, an illusion.

As we humans increasingly turn to lotteries and casinos hoping for the "big hit," we no longer honor the importance of long-range strategy. Instead, we spend our children's lunch money for a path through quicksand. This is a predictable road to real failure.

Not failure, but low aim, is a crime.

JAMES RUSSELL LOWELL

People are like stained glass windows; they sparkle and shine when the sun is out, but when the darkness sets in, their true beauty is revealed only if there is light within.

ELIZABETH KUBLER-ROSS

Failure either crushes a life or solidifies it. The wounded oyster mends its shell with a pearl.

ANONYMOUS

A word of encouragement during a failure is worth more than a whole book of praise after a success.

ANONYMOUS

Failure often breeds success. Football coaches Tom Landry, Chuck Noll, and Bill Walsh together won nine of the 16 Super Bowls in the years 1974 to 1989. Their teams — the Dallas Cowboys, Pittsburgh Steelers, and San Francisco 49ers — are regarded among the greatest ever, and Landry, Noll, and Walsh are considered among the best coaches the game has produced. This is well known. What is also a matter of record, but less well known, is that these three coaches also share the distinction of having three of the worst first-season records of any head coaches in National Football League history.

Business

These great coaches learned from their setbacks. Do you react to business reversals with denial, blaming others, or do you use setbacks to accept responsibility, analyze what misfired, and make the necessary changes for ultimate success?

Family

Thoreau said, "The mass of men lead lives of quiet desperation." Many families operate in the same manner. Are you helping to provide your family with meaning and purpose, or is everyone just going through the motions? Is your family operating with purpose or careening out of control? What are some signs that should give you an accurate answer?

Personal

Have you been devastated by what you consider personal failure: divorce, job, money, parenting? Have you given up or are you using this experience as a foundation for the future? Can you identify at least one friend who has suffered a tremendous personal loss who you can help?

COMMUNICATION

COMMUNICATION

Wolves are among the most social of carnivores. They don't rely upon any single form of communication but utilize every means at their disposal. They howl, nuzzle, lick, assume a dominant or submissive posture, utilize intricate body language — including lips, eyes, facial expressions, and tail position — or use scent to relay messages.

While many have heard that wolves' eyes glow in the dark, most of us are not aware that their eyes are used for the most sensitive of communications. Minuscule movements of the eye's musculature, as well as changes in pupil size, express surprise, fear, happiness, recognition, and other emotions.

Direct eye contact in the form of a fixed look or stare can be intimidating and is often interpreted as a threat by the wolf. When wolves want to signal friendliness and openness, they may gaze down or look away. When they are at ease and happy, wanting to play, you will see them display openness, expansiveness, and a "let's have some fun" attitude.

Because wolves are constantly facing life-and-death situations, effective communication is vital to the pack's survival. When on the attack, the situation changes by the second, and the wolves' intricate communication system allows them to constantly adjust their strategy and tactics to achieve success.

To wolves the art of communication is paying close attention to all types of communication, particularly body language. Their powers of observation are honed so finely that they record even the most subtle changes in each other's behavior.

When an adult wolf addresses a pup, it will drop its head in order to get on the pup's level and make puppy "whimper" sounds. In effect, it is saying, "OK, so I'm a big guy, but I'm on your level. I understand. I'm empathetic. We are all members of the same pack."

Most of the organizations I am privileged to work with as a consultant have leaders who realize that management skills and teamwork are not developed in one slam-bang session but come only as a result of regular, consistent effort over a period of time. At the first meeting I ask the executives and managers present to list in order of preference the qualities they would like to see improved in their organization.

Almost without exception, item number one will be trust, and second on the list will be communication. Experience has taught me that while it may sometimes be possible to have communication without having trust, it is impossible to have trust without clear communication. Families and other organizations can overcome their problems with open communication, but they become dysfunctional without it.

The ability of wolves to communicate so effectively and clearly with each other is probably one reason they so seldom actually fight each other to the death.

Could humans avoid much violence, misunderstanding, and failure if we worked as hard to develop and use competent communication skills as wolves do?

If you can see John Brown through John Brown's eyes, you can sell John Brown what John Brown buys.

RICH WILKINS

When the eyes say one thing and the tongue another, a practiced man relies on the language of the first.

RALPH WALDO EMERSON

The Great Spirit gave us two ears and one tongue so we can listen twice as much as we speak.

NATIVE AMERICAN PROVERB

The greatest problem in communication is the illusion that it has been accomplished.

GEORGE BERNARD SHAW

It is said that Prime Minister Winston Churchill had become very concerned about General Bernard Montgomery's lack of rapport with his troops. "Monty" did not like to associate with the men who did his fighting, preferring the company of the privileged and elite. Churchill called the general in for a chat and urged him to improve his communication with his men. Montgomery, typically adverse to advice from others, reportedly huffed, "Mr. Prime Minister, familiarity breeds contempt." Churchill, with a pull on his cigar and a splash of brandy, is said to have replied, "My dear General, without familiarity, there would be no breed."

Business

An overwhelming majority of top corporate executives say they believe that regular communication with employees improves job satisfaction and increases profits. However, fewer than one out of four of these same executives report that they actually engage in such communication. Do you talk one way but act another?

Family

Research reveals that most family members truly communicate with each other for only a few minutes during a week's time. Have you allowed your business or professional activities to shut out the ones you love? Which gets more of your attention at home — your family members or the TV set?

Personal

Effective communication is an art. While it comes easier for some more than others, it can be developed and improved by all of us. Do you encourage people to give you honest feedback on your communication skills, or do you just assume they are adequate? Videotaped encounters of your communication process can provide you with invaluable insight, particularly when combined with feedback from others. What are you doing to improve your techniques of communication?

PERSEVERANCE

PERSEVERANCE

Wolves have roamed this planet for more than one million years. Man has hunted, poisoned, trapped, and even shot them from helicopters and airplanes with high-powered weapons. Man has also destroyed much of the wolf's habitat as well as that of many of the herd animals like the bison, moose, and caribou which wolves have historically depended upon. Before the prosperity of man, wolves were the most widespread wild creatures in the world.

Still they persevere, roaming free in the more remote parts of our world. These are animals that want no handouts from man. They only desire to be left alone and allowed to live the way the Creator meant for them to exist. In a sad sense, the wolves' determination to preserve their social order and way of life resulted in their almost being wiped off the face of the earth. But while they must now adapt to some of the harshest climates and most rugged terrain on earth, they determinedly pursue their way of life.

Just as there are Alpha wolves, so too is there often an Omega wolf in the pack. This is usually, but not always, a male wolf and is often the runt of the litter. It can be painful to watch the pack seemingly mistreat this young member, relegating him to last place in almost everything, particularly getting to eat.

However, a strange phenomenon often emerges from this behavior. Omega wolves, when they survive, tend to become very tough critters. At some point they often begin giving every bit as good as they get. And it is not unusual that these Omega wolves, after proving their survivability, venture off on their own, becoming the proverbial "lone wolves" for a period of time. These lone wolves eventually join other packs or find a mate and begin a pack of their own.

In either case, the outcome of their stubborn perseverance is a positive for the world of wolves. If they join a new pack, they eventually inject new blood into the pack, mitigating the effects of inbreeding. If they become the Alpha leader of their own pack, the members of that pack have a leader that persevered against great odds and won.

We see the same outcome in many of our human organizations: the military recruit who is constantly harassed but becomes a terrific soldier; the ball player who is told he is too small but goes on to become a star; the child diagnosed with a learning disability who not only succeeds but triumphs by winning an academic scholarship to college. The list is endless, as are the characteristics of perseverance itself.

There is no substitute for perseverance in the life of the wolf, for it enables them to survive against all odds. Are we humans any different?

What would you attempt to do if you knew you could not fail?

DR. ROBERT SCHULLER

You miss 100 percent of the shots you never take.

WAYNE GRETZKY

Our greatest glory is not in never falling but in rising every time we fall.

CONFUCIUS

Perseverance is not a long race; it is many short races one after another.

WALTER ELLIOTT

Surveys show that people's greatest fear is speaking in public. Some of the best speakers I have ever heard are people who at one time could not stand before a crowd without uncontrollable fear. Whether it was sheer stage fright, stuttering, an inability to construct a decent presentation, or a feeling they were going to pass out, they realized that they were not competent public speakers. However, instead of giving up, they joined the Toastmasters organization and subjected themselves to regular doses of what they feared most, speaking in front of others. Through coaching, reassurance, and most of all perseverance, these people eventually became the golden-tongued orators most of us envy for talents that appear to be God-given. They are so good that we often do not realize that it was perseverance — not natural talent — that took them to the top.

Business

No amount of talent will replace the ability to persevere. Is this a characteristic your colleagues see you bring to every task you undertake, or is perseverance something you utilize only for the projects that suit your fancy?

Family

Perseverance is best taught by example. What specific examples of perseverance have you modeled for your family?

Personal

Some people persevere with determination while others are just plain stubborn. Do you know the difference?

STRATEGY

STRATEGY

Hunters, photographers, researchers, and others who have been fortunate enough to witness an actual wolf pack hunt often report being speechless when fate has had its way. Only moments before, as the observers peered through their binoculars, the wolves may have seemed to be aimlessly trailing the herd, as they had for days before. Suddenly, the apparently lethargic wolves spring into action as a coordinated, powerful, focused team, with each wolf understanding the strategic plan and the part they are to play.

There are endless variations of the strategies wolves use to accomplish their goal, but one account stands out in my mind. A team of four wolves suddenly began a coordinated charge on a herd of musk ox, driving them over a moderate rise. As the musk ox topped the rise, they were confronted by two wolves standing motionless directly in their path, looking immovable and emotionless. The musk ox panicked (as the wolves knew they would) scattering in all directions, thereby losing the protection the group afforded.

As the musk ox ran wildly in confusion, all six wolves converged on one elderly, somewhat feeble musk ox, no longer protected by its herd. One wolf attached itself to the animal's lower jaw, another to the forehead, pulling the prey to the ground as the other wolves literally took its legs out from under it. The struggle was quickly over. The musk ox had complacently relied on the group for protection and had no plan to contend with a skillfully executed attack. The wolf pack was small in comparison to the ox herd but had a strategy, executed it expertly, and won.

Unfortunately, when I first meet with a new management group, it is almost a given that few, if any of them, will know the mission or goals of their organization. Without this knowledge, there can be no coherent strategy. The same negative answer is often given when I ask them if they can state their personal goals and mission in life.

Without realizing it, have you adopted the philosophy of the old saying, "If you don't know where you are going, any road will get you there"?

The mightiest rivers lose their force when split up into several streams.

OVID, *LOVE'S CURE*

The best defensive strategy is the courage to attack yourself.

AL REIS

The executive must choose between using his power to strengthen the organization and using his power to strengthen his personal power base.

BRUCE HENDERSON

A strategy is trying to understand where you sit in today's world. Not where you wish you were or where you hoped you would be, but where you are. It's trying to understand where you want to be five years out. It's assessing the realistic chances of getting from here to there.

JOHN WELCH

Divide the fire, and you will the sooner put it out.

PUBLIUS SYRUS

Every organization, regardless of size, needs a strategic plan. Most organizations, particularly larger ones, have them. Every person, regardless of his or her situation, needs a strategic plan. Unfortunately, most do not have them. The problem with most formal strategic plans is that they are often placed on a bookshelf where they only collect dust. They work beautifully until either a crisis occurs or an opportunity arises. Managers looking for short-term results tend to make short-term decisions.

Managers with long-term goals are able to adapt short-term "surprises" to the organization's strategic plan, merging the two together rather than destroying one for the other.

Many people may remember the Tylenol disaster when people died because a crazed individual filled Tylenol capsules with poison. The positive lesson of that tragedy was the way the company responded. They didn't deny, lie, or shift blame. They were honest with the public, recalled their product, and re-engineered its packaging. Most people thought the company would not survive. They did. They stuck to their business and their product, and they did what was right. They believed that quality products and service would produce profits. They adhered to their long-term strategy, while implementing necessary short-term adjustments. They were not wrong. Tylenol is still number one, and as a bonus, tamper-proof packaging is now standard in the food and drug industry.

Business

Does your organization have a strategic plan? Do you know what it says? Does your plan really make any difference in your day-to-day decisions? Do your employees understand your strategic plan? If not, what do you need to do to make sure everyone is singing off the same sheet of music?

Family

Why did you have a family? Why didn't you remain single? What are the goals of your family? Do you set them or does everyone participate? Because plans need to be flexible, how does your family do a periodic reality check?

Personal

What method do you use to keep yourself on track in terms of the things you truly want to accomplish? Do you have your goals in writing? Do you reassess them monthly, yearly, or ever? You are the expert on you, so what is your strategy?

PLAY

PLAY

Humans routinely use the term "work hard, play hard," but this is the way wolves actually live. Wolf pups are exuberant, and their play is often uninhibited. Wolves are sociable animals that draw strength from physical contact with each other. Play refines their skills of communication, teamwork, and hunting.

But play serves other purposes. It provides a practical method of establishing and constantly reassessing the pecking order within the pack. Through experimental play, wolves learn how to acquire food and sustenance. They also become physically stronger and mentally tougher through play. So, for the wolf, play is not always just play.

Wolves realize that play is not just a by-product of life but a reason for life. Wolves' love of play is never exhausted, regardless of age. I have watched 15-year-old wolves play just as hard and have just as much fun as a litter of young pups. And since they have honed their game skills throughout their lifetime, they can often win while exerting less effort. Though they have matured, play is just as important in their lives as ever.

In the fast-track, downsized environment of today, many people think play is now superfluous to their lives — an activity they can no longer afford. Yet, when I interview a group of employees, I always hear, "I used to enjoy coming to work here. We had fun. Now it's all bottom line, serious, don't dare laugh or someone will think you are screwing off. So, I come to work, get through the day and get out of here at 5 p.m. If that's what they want, I'll give it to them."

In many families today, play no longer seems a viable option. The father and mother have busy, demanding careers that leave them exhausted at the end of the day, with no energy left for fun. They often travel extensively, removing them from most interaction with the family, much less "fun time." The husband and wife don't even play with each other any more — there are errands to run and always something else to do.

Does any of this ring a bell with you? Who has the right idea about the importance of play, the wolves or us?

Don't get so busy making a living that you don't know what you're living for.

UNKNOWN

In every person is hidden a child who wants to play.

HARVEY RUBEN

It should be noted that children's games are not merely games; one should regard them as their most serious activities.

MICHEL DE MONTAIGNE

People who cannot find time for recreation are obliged sooner or later to find time for illness.

UNKNOWN

Southwest Airlines is a company that seems to thrive on zaniness. Whether it is a creative Halloween costume proudly worn by a ticket seller, a goofy game for the passengers orchestrated by a flight attendant, or a spur-of-the-moment party for Southwest employees hosted by the airline's colorful chairman, Southwest means fun at work. I was recently aboard a Southwest flight that began with a flight attendant suddenly appearing hanging out of an overhead luggage rack to give the safety instructions. After everyone finally stopped laughing, the attendant began dispensing the safety tips — she had everyone's undivided attention.

Southwest also means success. This "low fare" airline has consistently won what they proudly term the Triple Crown Award. This is based on statistics from the Air Travel Consumer Report, which is put out by the Department of Transportation. Southwest regularly excels in (1) Best on-time performance, (2) Best luggage handling, and (3) Fewest customer complaints of all airlines. Fun at work and terrific customer service obviously go hand in hand.

Business

Is there a good reason why work can't also be productive play?
Does taking yourself so seriously improve your effectiveness
with co-workers or diminish it?

Family

Do you refer to the other members of your household as
"family" but treat them as inferiors? If you play together, do
you always find it necessary to keep score? Do you play with
family members for fun or to make a point?

Personal

Do you really practice the axiom that play can have a purpose
and be fun at the same time? When is the last time you had a
big belly-laugh at yourself? We are all ridiculous, so why not
acknowledge, cherish, and have fun with it?

DEATH AND SURVIVAL

DEATH AND SURVIVAL

W hen a wise human being dies, whether it be Aristotle, Confucius, Helen Keller, Winston Churchill, or the local barber who dispenses sage advice, society suffers. It is no different in the society of wolves. The death of an adult wolf can seriously jeopardize the entire pack. Knowledge of safe den sites in which to raise pups, game trails favored by quarry, or reliable watering holes may disappear with the loss of an elder wolf. The elimination of a key wolf means the sacrifice of years of experience, knowledge, and leadership ability.

Likewise, without proper preparation, the loss of a key executive can severely damage a company. A parent's death often either pulls the remaining members of the family closer together or begins a process of bickering and disintegration. Fortunately, the wolf pack elders constantly teach and mentor the younger wolves, giving them opportunities to fail, learn, and grow into positions of leadership.

The entire pack hunts, plays, and helps raise its pups together. All of these activities serve to reinforce the pack's social order and traditions. Younger wolves respect the unique gifts the elders possess, which is illustrated by the deference they show them. Therefore, the death of a single wise wolf, while damaging, is not usually fatal to the pack, for the younger wolves have been prepared well.

Nature's law of survival of the fittest continues to operate in the world of the wolf. Just as the weakest caribou are taken by the wolves, the weakest wolves also disappear. Human hunters often don't seem to understand this basic law, for they are intent on killing the biggest and strongest animals so they can mount the showiest, most impressive trophies.

It is natural survival in reverse. While limits are set on the number of wild animals we can kill, there are no limits or restrictions on taking the best of the breed. I don't ever remember hearing a hunter (myself included) say, "OK, let's go out and shoot the weak and the ill so the breed will be improved rather than minimized." And yet, this is exactly what wolves do when they hunt.

Could it be that to become more rational human beings,

we need to learn from the so-called "primitive" behavior of the wolf? How strange.

One very successful company I have worked with has a large banner hung over the entranceway that boldly proclaims, "Reward failure." This may seem strange at first, but when you understand the logic behind it, the simple wisdom is apparent. If no one fails, then no one is trying anything new, innovative, or different. This happens because people are afraid they will be punished if their efforts are not successful, so they play it safe and do things the way they have always done them. Meanwhile, the competition eats their lunch.

Encouraging risk taking may mean the death of one idea that didn't work, but the attitude and determination to improve will insure the long-term survival of the organization.

Reward failure!

Give a man a fish and you feed him for a day. Teach a man to fish and you feed him for a lifetime.

CHINESE PROVERB

The more we exploit nature, the more our options are reduced until we have only one: to fight for survival.

MORRIS UDALL

Death is not the enemy; living in constant fear of it is.

NORMAN COUSINS, *THE HEALING HEART*

How frighteningly few are the persons whose death would spoil our appetite and make the world seem empty.

ERIC HOFFER

Whether an organization is a business or family, the key to its long-term survival is the sharing of knowledge, information, and experience among the members. This process requires commitment, patience, and a visionary philosophy toward the group. An all-too-true parody portrays two executives discussing one of their employees. One executive says to the other, "He needs seasoning — fire him." The business culture of today is often short-term and shortsighted, basing success on quarterly earnings rather than long-term indicators of success. The viable organization, whether family or business, prizes training, coaching, compassion, and mentoring.

Business

What mechanisms are in place for the effective mentoring and transfer of knowledge from your experienced managers to your newer managers? Is this an integral part of your corporate culture? If so, how are managers rewarded for the effective development of people?

Family

Do you set aside time to pass along the knowledge that can insure survival of your family unit, or do you just count on osmosis to do the job? How much time each week do you spend communicating with family members? When specifically does this process take place?

Personal

Do you let others know that you would appreciate learning from them? Do you know that studies show that people who have mentors have more successful personal and professional lives? Are you willing to set aside your own ego to benefit from others' experiences?

LOYALTY

LOYALTY

No other mammal shows more spirited devotion to its family, organization, or social group than the wolf. The members of the wolf pack hunt together to insure survival of the group, but they also play, sing, sleep, scuffle, and protect each other. A wolf's purpose for existing is to insure the survival of the pack.

A wolf pack is made up of parents, aunts, uncles, brothers, sisters, half brothers, and half sisters — it is truly an extended family organization. And though generally only the Alpha male and Alpha female produce pups, every member of the pack participates in the nurturing and education of the young. Each pack member assumes responsibility for food, shelter, training, protection, and play where the pups are concerned, for the pack realizes that the young are their future.

The loyalty exhibited between wolves is well known and

documented. But a Montana man who has used his summers for years to study wolves in Alaska gave me a different view of wolf loyalty. He told about a couple he knew who lived in an extremely remote area with their two sons in a log cabin they had made by hand. This family also included two wolves they had raised from earliest puppyhood, rescuing them from their den after their mother had been indiscriminately shot and the pups left to die. This was the only family the wolves had ever known, having only lived with humans as their pack mates.

One day the parents were cutting wood about a mile from home when one of the boys accidentally turned over a kerosene lamp (there was no electricity), and a raging fire began to consume the wooden structure. The two wolves immediately dashed toward the flaming cabin where the two boys were trapped inside, immobilized by smoke and fear. The parents were far behind, so the wolves gnawed and fought their way into the cabin and pulled the boys outside to safety. Though both wolves were badly burned, their loyalty to their "pack" meant the difference between life and death for these two members of their "pack."

If the leaders of organizations, whether the organization is a family or a company, do not really believe in the importance of education and personal and management development of their members, then neither will anyone else. There should be no tolerance of the attitude that continuing education is just a "soft cost" that can be harmlessly cut to boost profits or reduce expenses with no long-term negative effects to the organization. Giving people the opportunity and tools to improve themselves builds the type of loyalty that is an asset of inestimable worth to both the individual and the organization.

Men exist for the sake of one another.
MARCUS AURELIUS

In the final analysis, it is not what you do for your children but what you have taught them to do for themselves that makes them successful human beings.
ANN LANDERS

Loyalty means not that I agree with everything you say or that I believe you are always right. Loyalty means that I share a common ideal with you and that, regardless of minor differences, we fight for it, shoulder to shoulder, confident in one another's good faith, trust, constancy, and affection.
DR. KARL A. MENNINGER

He has every characteristic of a dog except loyalty.
HENRY FONDA, *THE BEST MAN*

Many employers and employees alike seem to believe there is no longer any such thing as loyalty, at least in the traditional sense, but few seem sure what to do about the situation. The answer may lie in the fact that we are entering a new era of opportunity and self-reliance. There may be very few "25 years of service" gold watches awarded in the future, but a new type of loyalty, born through the process of cross-training and re-engineering can be superior in many ways. We should promote employability instead of guaranteed employment. It is counterproductive to waste words proclaiming a company to be a "family." It is a business, and there is no reason to camouflage the fact. The goal, instead, should be to develop the most highly trained, flexible, innovative, cross-trained employees in your industry. The result will be a new type of loyalty that can thrive on the waves of change we all experience.

Business

Are you preparing your employees to survive in any economic climate, anywhere, anytime? If you do, you will build a new brand of devotion and loyalty — and superior employees.

Family

People in all types of organizations are most devoted to goals they help set. Does your family operate as a unit, interdependently, or do you attempt to unilaterally set the course for everyone?

Personal

To receive devotion and loyalty, it is essential that we give it. Just what is it you are willing to commit to, without reservation, in your life? Are your actual priorities the ones you say they are?

CHANGE

CHANGE

Wolves' ability to manage change is a major reason why they, along with humans, are among the most successful and durable mammals in the world. For instance, wolves seem to practice a type of natural population control, automatically curtailing or escalating their reproductive rate in relation to the prey and space available. While we blissfully ignore the fact that the world's human population is careening out of control, the wolf pack continues to live in balance with nature. How much better would the odds of the world continuing to survive be if humans would adopt this technique?

Often the proverbial "lone wolf" — the runt, outcast, or rebel of a pack — will join another pack, perhaps after thousands of miles of treacherous travel and painful rejections. When a pack's numbers have become low or there is a need for an injection of "new blood" into the pack's genetic base, the lone wolf is welcomed into the fold.

The constant movement and evolution of the world's land mass throughout the centuries, as well as the exploding intrusion of humans, particularly in the last 200 years, has dramatically altered the types of herds and animals available to both wolves and people. Whether the herds have been caribou, elk, moose, or white-tailed deer, the wolf has skillfully adjusted to what was available and hunted accordingly.

But when I speak to conventions and corporate groups, I stress that our greatest lesson from wolves may be in what they refuse to change. Their lives epitomize loyalty, teamwork, and interdependence. They take care of their young and their elderly as well. They know what is important to them, and they are prepared to fight to hold on to it. They are adaptable animals in terms of geography and prey, but their values are never compromised. A wolf pack seems to survive as well eating the now-abundant white-tailed deer as it can on moose, caribou, or elk, which are no longer plentiful in many regions. This change they can accept, but wolves cannot survive if they do not nurture, educate, and protect their young and constantly put the welfare of the pack first. This is their essence, and this they refuse to change.

Not everything that is faced can be changed. But nothing can be changed until it is faced.

JAMES BALDWIN

Nature is the most thrifty thing in the world, she never wastes anything; she undergoes change, but there's no annihilation — the essence remains.

T. BINNEY

Nature's mighty law is change.

ROBERT BURNS

The only person who likes change is a wet baby.

ROY BLITZER

Thanks to Federal Express, the overnight letter became a symbol of great innovation in the 1980s. This was truly a revolutionary change. Next came the fax machine, allowing us to quickly send documents down the street, across town, or around the world. Today, most of us are talking to each other using e-mail, while conducting business and doing research or a multitude of other tasks over the Internet. As magnificent as these changes have been, they are still only tools. It is the adherence to our values, regardless of the tools we use to implement them, that will bring us success.

Business

Do you sponsor change, or just endure it? What changes have you initiated in your business in the last year? What one major change could revolutionize your company?

Family

Your family members are constantly exposed to shifting societal values. If adopted, many of these behaviors are disastrous to individuals and families. Do you address these issues with your family, or do you prefer to act like the ostrich, believing these potential pitfalls only affect other families?

Personal

Participants in my management development programs are asked confidentially if they welcome or avoid change. Overwhelmingly, they answer that they thrive on change. Paradoxically, their CEO often views the situation differently, perceiving that the managers are determined to preserve the old order.

Are you honest with yourself about how you respond to changes that others initiate?

Are you certain of your own values? What makes you and your organization unique? What is your reason for existing? Do you know what you are willing to change in life and what you will fight to hold on to if threatened?

CONCLUSION

CONCLUSION

The caves of the world have yielded a vast amount of information about prehistoric man. Scholars have delighted in interpreting the paintings discovered in these caves. One often overlooked fact is that early man seldom drew paintings of people, preferring instead to focus on the animals he observed daily in his quest to survive. The wolf is one of the most frequently portrayed animals in these paintings.

No one knows why the emphasis was on animals, rather than man. Could it be that early man saw himself as a participant in this world, along with animals, rather than as the sole proprietor? There was much to learn from the animals, for they knew how to endure the cold and exist in a hostile environment. Early man very well may have found animals more interesting than himself, a difficult concept in this age of self-indulgence and instant gratification.

Ancient man did not view animals as inferiors but as partners in nature's intricate ecosystem. Wolves were respected for their wisdom and other particular gifts which we are once again rediscovering.

As Bernard Baruch said, "We didn't all come over in the same ship, but we're all in the same boat."

Two roads diverged in a wood and I took the one less traveled — and that has made all the difference.

ROBERT FROST

Sooner or later every one of us breathes an atom that has been breathed before by anyone you can think of who has lived before us — Michelangelo or George Washington or Moses.

JACOB BRONOWSKI

There is no security on this earth; there is only opportunity.

DOUGLAS MACARTHUR

For all things share the same breath — the beast, the trees, the man, they all share the same breath. . . .

What is man without the beasts?

If all the beasts were gone, man would die from a great loneliness of spirit. For whatever happens to the beasts soon happens to man.

All things are connected. . . . Whatever befalls the earth befalls the sons of the earth.

CHIEF SEATTLE, 1854

EPILOGUE

EPILOGUE

As a speaker and consultant, I have the unique privilege of being able to observe the delicate human interactions that take place within today's sophisticated organizations. How these interactions are handled often determines the ultimate success or failure of these groups, whether they be businesses, hospitals, governmental units, non-profit associations, or family units. The same principles work for all.

Too often trust and respect between management and employees have been replaced by cynicism and hostility. The day of the "twenty-fifth anniversary watch" being awarded is gone, with employees casually switching jobs and companies often changing ownership. A frequent lament I hear in today's workplace, among all levels of employees, goes like this: "I may as well be selling ball bearings or scrap metal as working in this so called professional job — all this organization cares about is money". Among corporate officials the feelings are reciprocal: "There's no such thing as loyalty anymore — after teaching executives the business, they leave you at the drop of a hat and join a competitor for a few bucks more a month and a handful of stock options."

Rather than just commiserate with people, I decided to do my part to help bring about some positive solutions. The implementation of Total Quality Management (TQM) programs, focus groups, interdepartmental teams, and other innovative techniques is a step in the right direction. But they often fizzle out for various reasons — insufficient involvement from the top, absence of true organizational commitment, lack of consistent application, overly complicated and cumbersome crisis management, and many others. As an independent advisor, I can only make recommendations concerning these issues which may or may not be heeded.

However, there are two variables I realized I could personally do something about — rewards and education. Managers today routinely encourage their employees to serve on various forms of interdepartmental teams, and these groups often achieve dramatic success. Repeatedly I have been able to help engineer these successes, only to observe everyone become mute when the subject arises as to how to reward employees for these extraordinary efforts. People seem at a loss to know how to reward their employees with something of lasting value, reinforce the company's operating philosophy, and, at the same time, use this opportunity to contribute to the employees' continuing management development.

These are just some of the goals we hope to accomplish when we reward people, and the challenge is almost always to do this without spending a lot of money. This relatively inexpensive book and the ones to follow provide a way to reward people, while reinforcing desirable values and an enlightened operating philosophy.

I have learned the importance of employee education and management development. After years of working with managers and executives at all levels in many different industries, I have decided that the metaphor or parable is by far the most effective teaching technique. People learn best by stories that have meaning, not by lectures. The more enjoyable, understandable, memorable, or even humorous the metaphor, the greater the transference of knowledge.

The result of these considerations was this book, *The Wisdom Of Wolves*. This is the first in a series of books utilizing the characteristics of animals as metaphors to help us understand our own lives and possibilities. The response to this first book about wolves has confirmed my belief that this is a relevant and fascinating subject for practically everyone. It is truly impossible to learn about wolves without also learning more about ourselves and the world around us.

My happiest surprises have come from learning of the many groups other than business organizations that have "bonded" with *The Wisdom Of Wolves*. Schools, churches, Boy Scout troops, camps, and numerous other groups have found ingenious ways to use the book for the benefit of their members, including not only reading the book but also using it as a fund-raiser to support their groups' values.

By using the wolf as a metaphor for our lives and organizational behavior, people not only learn valuable principles but also have a great time in the process. The lessons of the wolf pack visually demonstrate a management philosophy that every organization should want to foster among its members.

This is why I wrote this book and use the wolf metaphor in my speeches and seminars. People enjoy them. People learn from them, and I learn from the people. We all benefit. It is my humble attempt to "leave my mark."

For More Information

Following is a partial list of organizational and publications dedicated to the understanding and preservation of the wolf:

Canadian Wolf Defenders
3819-112A Street
Edmonton, Alberta, Canada T6J 1K4

Defenders of Wildlife
1244 19th Street NW
Washington, DC 20036-2266

Friends of Wolves, Ltd.
5706 3 Mile Road
Racine, WI 53406

Fund for Animals, Inc.
850 Sligo Avenue
Silver Springs, MD 20910

Green Wolf of Canada
429 Merten Street
Toronto, Ontario, Canada M4S 1B3

H.O.W.L. (Help Our Wolves Live)
4600 Emerson Avenue South
Minneapolis, MN 55409

HOWLERS
160 N. Fairview Avenue South
Minneapolis, MN 55409

International Wolf Center/*International Wolf Magazine*
1396 Highway 169
Ely, MN 55731

Julian Center for Science and Education
P.O. Box 1189
Julian, CA 92036

National Wildlife Federation
1400 Sixteenth Street, NW
Washington, DC 20036-2266

The Wolf Fund
The Center for the Humanities and the Environment
Box 471
Moose, WY 83012

Wolf Haven America
3111 Offut Lake Road
Tenino, WA 98589

The Wolf Recovery Foundation
P. O. Box 793
Boise, ID 83701

Wolf Song of Alaska
P. O. Box 110309
Anchorage, AK 99511-0309

The following references have been a great help to me in understanding the world of wolves. If you desire to learn more about wolves, I recommend these publications as an excellent way to continue your journey:

Brandenberg, Jim. *Brother Wolf: A Forgotten Promise*. Monocqua, WI: North Word Press, Inc., 1993.

Jenkins, Ken L. *Wolf Reflections*. Merrillville, IN: ICS Brooks, Inc., 1996.

Lawrence, R.D. *In Praise of Wolves*, New York: Henry Holt, 1986.

Lopez, Barry Holstun. *Of Wolves and Men*. New York: Scribner's, 1978.

Masson, Jeffrey Moussaleff and Susan McCarthy. *When Elephants Weep*. New York: Delacorte Press, 1995.

Mech, L. David. *Way of the Wolf*. Stillwater, MN: Voyageur Press, 1995.

Murray, John A. *Out Among the Wolves*. Seattle: Alaska Northwest Books, 1993.

Nature Company, *The Wolf: Spirit of the Wild*. San Francisco: Walking Stick Press, 1993.

Phillips, Michael K. and Douglass W. Smith. *The Wolves of Yellowstone*, Stillwater, MN: Voyageur Press, 1996.

Simon, Seymour. *Wolves*. New York: Trophy, 1995.

Wood, Daniel. *Wolves*. Vancouver: Whitecap Books, 1994.

ABOUT THE AUTHOR

T wyman L. Towery, Ph.D., is a professional speaker and consultant. His non-traditional management approach, with stunning audio-visuals, is effective with any type of audience. His presentations are always customized, relaxed, humorous, and full of cutting-edge content. He presents nationwide to all types of businesses and organizations. For more information, contact:

Twyman Towery
Towery Communications
141 Rue de Grande
Brentwood, TN 37027
Phone: 615-370-3587
Fax: 615-661-8944
E-mail: twyman@twymantowery.com